This
Lana
Book
Belongs to

BLUE
JEANS

YOUNG
AND
BEAUTIFUL

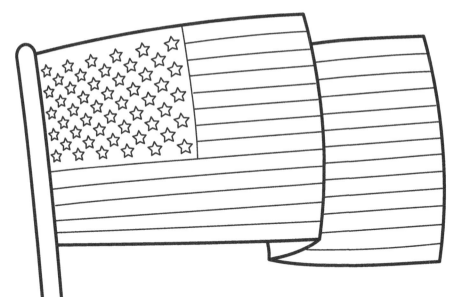

I'm your
National
Anthem

It's All So Sweet, Like
CINNAMON

BABY, PUT ON HEART-SHAPED

SUNGLASSES

I'VE BEEN OUT ON THAT OPEN ROAD

They say that the world

was built for two

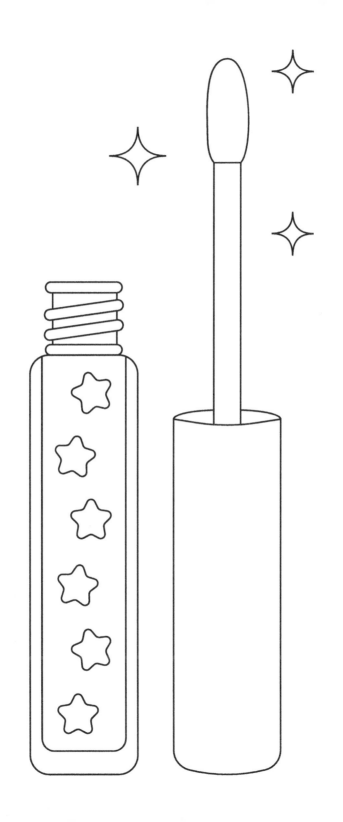

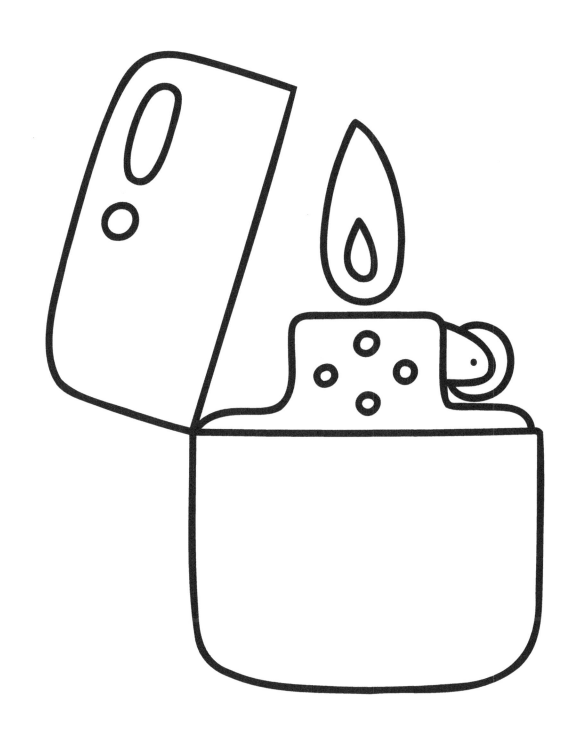

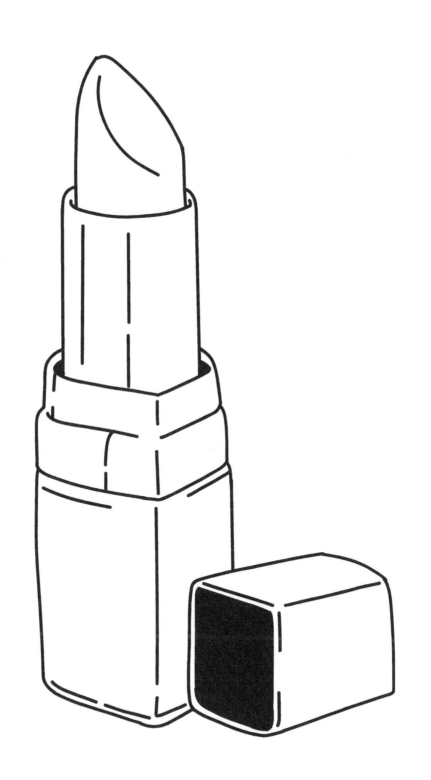

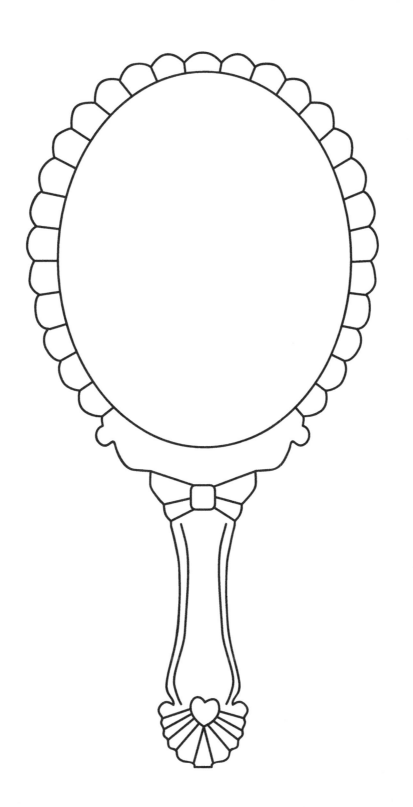

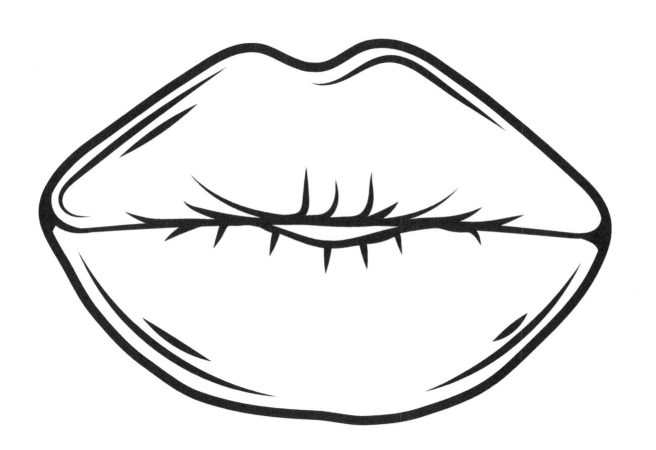

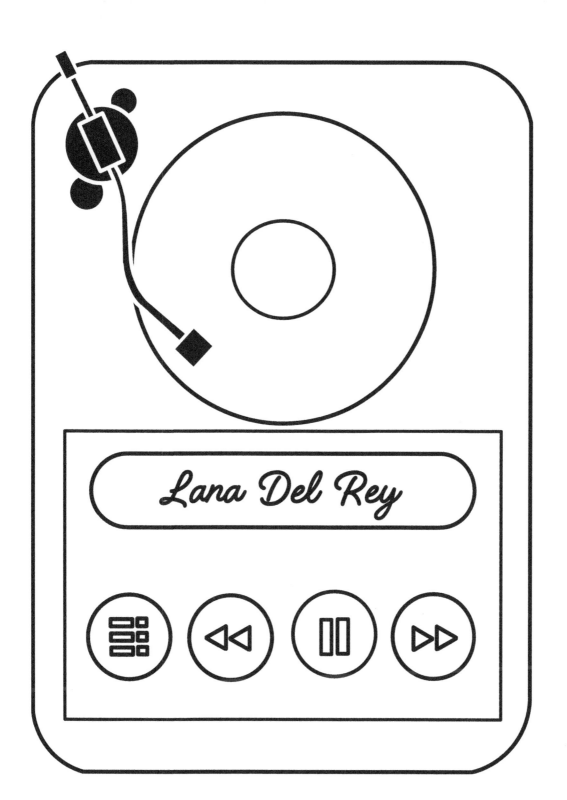

Made in the USA
Las Vegas, NV
31 March 2025

20365292R00070